Copyright © 2026 by Kevin Brady

ISBN: 978-1-971407-00-5

All rights reserved. No part of this publication may be reproduced, distributed, or transmitted in any form or by any means, including photocopying, recording, or other electronic or mechanical methods, without the prior written permission of the publisher, except in the case of brief quotations embodied in critical reviews and certain other noncommercial uses permitted by copyright law.

Scripture Quotations: Unless otherwise noted, all Scripture quotations are taken from the Holy Bible, New International Version®, NIV®. Copyright © 1973, 1978, 1984, 2011 by Biblica, Inc.™ Used by permission of Zondervan.

All rights reserved worldwide. www.zondervan.com. The "NIV" and "New International Version" are trademarks registered in the United States Patent and Trademark Office by Biblica, Inc.™

No portion of this book may be reproduced in any form without written permission from the publisher or author, except as permitted by U.S. copyright law.

Contents

1. Each Day Brings A New Promise — 1
2. Dedication — 2
3. Introduction — 3
4. Let Us Begin — 6
5. God's Faithfulness Each Morning — 8
6. Day 1: New Mercies Every Morning — 12
7. Day 2: The Light Will Break Through — 15
8. Day 3: Daily Bread, Daily Trust — 18
9. Day 4: Morning Brings His Voice — 21
10. Day 5: The Path Is Lit — 24
11. Day 6: His Presence Is Near — 27
12. Sunday 1: Resting in Faithfulness — 30
13. A New Creation in Christ — 32
14. Day 7: Made New — 36
15. Day 8: Clothed in Christ — 39

16.	Day 9: A Heart Transplant	42
17.	Day 10: A Mind Made New	45
18.	Day 11: From Shame to Grace	48
19.	Day 12: The Spirit's Seal	50
20.	Sunday Reflection: Resting in Renewal	52
21.	Joy in the Morning	54
22.	Day 13: Joy Comes in the Morning	58
23.	Day 14: Strength in Singing	61
24.	Day 15: Delight Over Despair	64
25.	Day 16: Joy in Trials	67
26.	Day 17: Fullness of Joy	69
27.	Day 18: The Oil of Gladness	72
28.	Sunday Reflection: Resting in Joy	75
29.	Hope and Light for a New Day	77
30.	Day 19: Hope That Anchors	81
31.	Day 20: Light in Darkness	84
32.	Day 21: The Morning Star	87
33.	Day 22: Future Glory	90
34.	Day 23: Mercy and Compassion	93
35.	Day 24: Radiant with Hope	95

36.	Sunday Reflection: Resting in Hope	98
37.	Living the Promise	100
38.	Day 25: Walking in the Light	104
39.	Day 26: Faith in Action	107
40.	Day 27: The Peaceful Path	110
41.	Day 28: Bearing Fruit That Lasts	113
42.	Day 29: The Strength of Service	116
43.	Day 30: Abiding in Love	119
44.	Sunday Reflection: Resting in Promise	122
45.	Day 31: The Promise Continues	124
46.	ABOUT THE AUTHOR	127

Each Day Brings A New Promise

A Sunrise Inspired 31-Day Devotional

By Kevin Brady

With gratitude to Pastor Brady Blasdel, who recognizes the talent and Spirit in me and challenges me to use it for the glory of God; and to Pastor José Flores, who shows me that the Holy Spirit transcends language, culture, and worldly things.

Dedication

For Alma, my beloved wife, and for our daughters, Katherine and Samantha — may you always awaken each morning with joy, knowing that God's promises are new every day.

Introduction

Each sunrise is more than a change in the sky; it is God's gentle reminder of His faithfulness. The night gives way to light, and with it comes the assurance that His mercies are new every morning (Lamentations 3:22–23).

No matter the burdens of yesterday, the dawn declares: God is not finished with you.

This devotional was written to help you begin each new day with hope, strength, and trust in God's promises. Every reading follows a rhythm of Scripture, Reflection, Application, and Prayer. Scripture anchors us in truth, Reflection opens our hearts to God's voice, Application offers practical steps, and Prayer draws us nearer to Him.

Suggested Use

- Daily Reading: Start each morning with a devotional to set the tone for your day.

- Journaling: Keep a notebook to capture how God speaks to you through each reflection.

- Prayer Focus: Use the applications as guides for prayer throughout your day.

Schedule Framework

30 daily devotionals: Six per week (Monday-Saturday) with Sunday as a day of renewal and reflection.

Day 31 (Monday) "The Promise Continues" — the invitation to begin again

How to Begin

Every journey with God begins with a simple *yes*. Before you turn to the first page of this devotional, take a deep breath and give Him your yes — your willingness to meet Him in the quiet of each morning.

Find a place where light can touch you — a favorite chair by the window, the porch, or the corner of a room that catches dawn. Bring your coffee, your Bible, or simply your open heart. You don't need anything more than attention and honesty.

Begin by praying a short invitation:

"Lord, I'm here. Meet me in this moment. Speak through Your Word, and let this day begin with You."

Read slowly. Let each Scripture settle before moving to the reflection. Pause whenever a line stirs something in you — joy, conviction, peace. That's where God is speaking.

End with gratitude. Write one line in your journal that begins, *"Today I see Your faithfulness in …"*

These small acknowledgments become seeds of joy for the next morning.

If you miss a day, don't chase the schedule — return to the sunrise in front of you. God's mercy is not measured in dates but in presence.

Each page of this book is an invitation, not a requirement.

Meet God where you are, as you are. The rest will rise like light.

Let Us Begin

A Morning Prayer for Beginning the Journey

Dear God, Lord of new mornings, thank You for inviting me into this rhythm of mercy and light. Quiet the noise around me so I can hear Your voice within me. Open my heart to wonder, my mind to truth, and my hands to what You place before me today. Let each sunrise remind me that You are near, and that every beginning with You is good. Amen.

Sunrise over a Lake in Texas

God's Faithfulness Each Morning

WEEK 1

Devotionals for the week:

Day	Title	Scripture	Theme
1	New Mercies Every Morning	Lamentations 3:22–23	Daily mercy and renewal
2	The Light Will Break Through	Psalm 30:5	Joy follows sorrow
3	Daily Bread, Daily Trust	Matthew 6:11	Dependence on God
4	Morning Brings His Voice	Psalm 5:3	Listening and prayer
5	The Path Is Lit	Psalm 119:105	Guidance through the Word
6	His Presence Is Near	Psalm 145:18	God's nearness
(Sunday)	Resting in Faithfulness	Exodus 33:14	Rest in His presence

Devotionals for Week 1

Pause and reflect with a song chosen to accompany the devotionals for this week.

QR Code for the Devotional Song to accompany Week 1

God's Faithfulness Each Morning

Day 1: New Mercies Every Morning

Scripture

"The steadfast love of the Lord never ceases; his mercies never come to an end; they are new every morning; great is your faithfulness."
—Lamentations 3:22–23

Lesson

When Jeremiah wrote these words, Jerusalem was in ruins and hope seemed gone. Yet, even while surrounded by ashes, he looked toward the dawn and declared that God's mercy was still alive. The city's walls were broken, but God's covenant was not.

Every sunrise carries that same quiet miracle. No matter how dark the night has been—regret, exhaustion, fear—the light slips through the blinds and whispers, *"You get to begin again."* God doesn't hand you a scorecard when you wake; He hands you mercy, freshly prepared for this very day.

Yesterday's failures have no authority over today's grace. God's love is not recycled; it's renewed—custom-made for the challenges, choices, and chances of this morning.

Reflection

Pause and notice the rhythm of creation: darkness to light, night to morning, endings to beginnings. That rhythm is the heartbeat of redemption. The same God who turns night into day can turn sorrow into strength and weariness into worship.

Ask yourself: *Where have I seen His mercy dawn before?* Perhaps in forgiveness you didn't deserve, peace that surprised you, or strength you couldn't explain. Each moment was a sunrise of grace, reminding you that His faithfulness outlasts your failures.

Application

- Before you check your phone or calendar, whisper a prayer of gratitude for a new start.

- Write down one mercy you've already experienced this morning—breath, warmth, forgiveness, possibility.

- Offer that same mercy to someone else today: a word of kindness, patience, or understanding.

- Commit to taking a moment each morning to receive God's word and blessing.

Prayer

Lord, thank You for meeting me with new mercies before I even asked for them. Wash away the weight of yesterday and awaken my spirit to Your presence today. Let every thought, word, and step reflect the freshness of Your grace. Renew my heart like the morning light—steady, gentle, and full of promise. Amen.

Today's Promise

God's faithfulness never sleeps—every sunrise is proof that grace begins again.

Day 2: The Light Will Break Through

Scripture

"Weeping may stay for the night, but rejoicing comes in the morning." — Psalm 30:5

Lesson

David knew what it was to walk through the long night of the soul—betrayal, loss, and silence from heaven. Yet he also knew that no night lasts forever. Joy is not delayed—it's *promised.* The same God who holds the stars in place also schedules your sunrise.

Tears may visit for a night, but they are not permanent residents. When you awaken, the light does more than reveal—it heals. The shadows that seemed endless in the dark lose their power when morning arrives, and the heart remembers: God has not forgotten you.

Reflection

Even in sorrow, the seeds of joy are being watered by your tears. What if the night you fear is simply preparing your eyes to appreciate the dawn?

Begin your morning by thanking Him for the joy He's already preparing.

Application

- Reflect on a time God brought you through a difficult night.
- Encourage someone who is still in their night.
- Choose joy as your response today.

Prayer

Lord, thank You for being the God who turns darkness into dawn. When I cannot see the light, help me trust that it is on its way. Let hope rise with the morning and joy awaken my soul. Amen.

Today's Promise

No night lasts forever—God's joy always finds the morning.

Day 3: Daily Bread, Daily Trust

Scripture

"Give us today our daily bread." — Matthew 6:11

Lesson

When Jesus taught His disciples this prayer, He was not giving them words to recite — He was teaching them the rhythm of dependence. His audience would have remembered the manna that fell each morning in the wilderness (Exodus 16). God's people gathered just enough for the day; anything extra spoiled overnight. It was a daily reminder that provision was tied to trust, not accumulation.

In a world that measures success by what can be stored, Christ invites us into a slower economy — one defined by sufficiency rather than surplus. When He says, *"Give us today our daily bread,"* He calls us to acknowledge our limits and His limitless care. The Father doesn't withhold tomorrow's portion; He simply asks that we meet Him in today's moment to receive it.

The sunrise reminds us that God's generosity renews with time itself. Each new light is fresh evidence that grace remains punctual. Worry often arrives early; provision always arrives right on schedule.

Reflection

What would your heart look like if you believed "enough" was holy?

Application

- Begin your day by asking God for today's grace — no more, no less.
- Replace every anxious "what if" with "thank You for what is."
- Close your evening by naming one small provision that met you right on time.

Prayer

Father, teach me the peace of daily dependence. Feed me with what I need, and free me from fearing what I don't. Amen.

Today's Promise

God's provision comes in daily portions — never too late, never too little.

Day 4: Morning Brings His Voice

Scripture

"In the morning, Lord, You hear my voice; in the morning I lay my requests before You and wait expectantly." — Psalm 5:3

Lesson

David wrote these words surrounded by danger and distraction. The Hebrew verb translated *"lay"* carries the sense of arranging — like a priest carefully setting sacrifices upon the altar. Each morning, David positioned his concerns before

God and waited for divine response. Prayer for him wasn't an emergency call; it was a morning appointment.

We often speak to God hoping for instant feedback, but Scripture models something deeper — worshipful waiting. Morning is not just when we pray; it's when we pause long enough to notice the God who already listened during the night. Stillness becomes sacred space, and expectancy becomes faith in motion.

When you begin your day by arranging your thoughts before the Lord, you shift the day's center of gravity. The rush remains, but the hurry leaves. Sunrise prayer doesn't shorten the to-do list. It sanctifies it.

Reflection

How might your day change if you spoke less and listened more in your prayer time?

Application

- Start one morning this week with silence before words.
- Write down three requests and place them somewhere visible as a reminder of surrender.
- End your prayer by waiting — not wondering if He hears but expecting that He will act.

Prayer

Lord, make me patient enough to hear before I move. Let my mornings become altars where Your wisdom meets my waiting. Amen.

Today's Promise

The God who listens through the night speaks at dawn.

Day 5: The Path Is Lit

Scripture

"Your word is a lamp for my feet, a light on my path." — Psalm 119:105

Lesson

Psalm 119 is the longest chapter in Scripture — a poetic map of what life looks like when guided by divine instruction. In the ancient world, travelers carried small clay lamps that cast just enough light for their next few steps. The psalmist's metaphor reminds us that God's Word rarely floods the horizon; it simply reveals what's next.

We often wish for full visibility, but God offers proximity instead. The lamp is sufficient because His presence is near. When the next turn looks uncertain, the light of Scripture gives both direction and companionship. Every obedient step creates space for the next beam of revelation to appear.

Patience in the journey is an act of worship. Faith walks forward, even when vision feels partial, trusting that the One who lit the path will finish the road.

Reflection

Are you waiting for clarity when God has already given you enough light to take the next step?

Application

- Act on the last clear instruction God gave you — even if you can't see the outcome.
- Carry one verse in your mind today as your "lamp."
- Thank Him tonight for each step He illuminated only when you needed it.

Prayer

Guide of my steps, shine enough for faith to follow, and no more than I can handle. Keep me walking in the rhythm of Your light. Amen.

Today's Promise

Obedience turns limited light into endless guidance.

Day 6: His Presence Is Near

Scripture

"The Lord is near to all who call on Him, to all who call on Him in truth." — Psalm 145:18

Lesson

This psalm, David's final one, is a sweeping declaration of God's character. After a life filled with both triumph and regret, he closes his story not by boasting of victories but by celebrating God's nearness. In Hebrew, *"near"* suggests both proximity and readiness — God not only dwells close but leans in when His people speak honestly.

We sometimes measure faith by emotion, but David measures it by attention. God is not more present in moments of ecstasy than in ordinary hours; He is simply more noticed. Calling on Him "in truth" doesn't mean flawlessly — it means sincerely. Honesty opens the distance between heaven and earth until there is none left.

Morning prayer reminds us that we don't have to climb toward God; He has already descended toward us. The presence we seek is the presence that's already seeking us.

Reflection

How would your prayer change if you began it with awareness instead of effort?

Application

- Begin each prayer time by pausing to acknowledge, *"You are here."*

- Throughout the day, whisper a brief thank-you instead of long requests.

- Before bed, reflect on one moment you sensed His quiet nearness.

Prayer

God who draws near, teach me that awareness is worship. Let Your presence become the atmosphere of my day. Amen.

Today's Promise

Nearness isn't something God achieves.

It's who He already is.

Sunday 1: Resting in Faithfulness

Scripture:

"My presence will go with you, and I will give you rest." — Exodus 33:14

Reflection:
Pause before the next sunrise.
Today is not for progress but presence.
Let quietness remind you …

that God's faithfulness is not proven by your pace,
but by His steady nearness.
Rest is not the absence of work …

it's the awareness of God at work within you.

A New Creation in Christ
Week 2

Devotionals for the week

Day	Title	Scripture	Theme
7	Made New	2 Corinthians 5:17	Identity and rebirth
8	Clothed in Christ	Galatians 3:27	Righteous covering
9	A Heart Transplant	Ezekiel 36:26	Spiritual renewal
10	A Mind Made New	Romans 12:2	Transformation through truth
11	From Shame to Grace	Psalm 34:5	Freedom from shame
12	The Spirit's Seal	Ephesians 1:13	Belonging and assurance
(Sunday)	Resting in Renewal	Isaiah 40:31	Strength through waiting

Devotionals for Week 2

Scan and Listen to a song chosen to accompany the devotionals for this week.

Week 2 QR Code for Music to accompany this week's devotionals

A New Creation in Christ

Day 7: Made New

Scripture

"Therefore, if anyone is in Christ, the new creation has come: the old has gone, the new is here." — 2 Corinthians 5:17

Lesson

When Paul wrote to the church in Corinth, he addressed believers caught between two worlds — the values of their culture and the call of Christ. Corinth was a city of success and indulgence, a place that celebrated status more than sanctification. Paul's words cut through their confusion with a declaration: the moment you belong to Christ; you are no longer who you were.

He wasn't describing a gradual self-improvement plan. He was describing a spiritual resurrection. "The old has gone" doesn't mean forgotten; it means crucified. In its place stands something holy — not patched up, but reborn. The Spirit of God moves into the soul and writes a new beginning.

For you, this verse isn't theory — it's your biography. You are not a slightly better version of your past; you are the living proof that death has lost its hold, and grace has the final word.

Reflection

Where in your life is God inviting you to stop renovating the old and start embracing the new?

Application

- Speak life over yourself today: *"In Christ, I am new."*

- Identify one area still shaped by the "old self" and surrender it in prayer.

- Celebrate visible signs of change, however small — they are resurrection in motion.

Prayer

Lord Jesus, thank You that my old life is made new in You. Teach me to walk as one reborn, not improved — a living testimony of Your grace. Amen.

Today's Promise

God doesn't restore who you were; He reveals who you've become.

Day 8: Clothed in Christ

Scripture

"For all of you who were baptized into Christ have clothed yourselves with Christ." — Galatians 3:27

Lesson

Paul's letter to the Galatians reminded believers who were tangled in legalism that salvation was never about performance — it was about position. Baptism symbolized their union with Christ, and to be "clothed" with Him meant that His righteousness now covered their entire being.

In ancient times, new clothing marked a change in identity — a rite of passage or a new allegiance. Paul used that imagery intentionally: when you come to Christ, you are no longer defined by your past, your failures, or your social standing. You wear grace. You are robed in righteousness not your own.

The beauty of being clothed in Christ is that you don't put Him on and take Him off; you live wrapped in His presence. You walk into every moment with divine covering, carrying His light like a garment that never fades.

Reflection

What have you been wearing that no longer fits who you are in Christ — shame, fear, guilt, or pride?

Application

- Each morning, as you dress, whisper: *"I am clothed in Christ today."*

- Let compassion and humility be your visible garments.

- Thank God for the protection and identity found in His righteousness.

Prayer

Father, thank You for wrapping me in Your grace. Let my life reflect the beauty of belonging to You. Amen.

Today's Promise

You are covered, not concealed — clothed in the confidence of grace.

Day 9: A Heart Transplant

Scripture

"I will give you a new heart and put a new spirit in you; I will remove from you your heart of stone and give you a heart of flesh." — Ezekiel 36:26

Lesson

Ezekiel spoke these words to Israel during exile — a people who had hardened themselves through rebellion. God promised not just to forgive them but to transform them from within. Their problem wasn't circumstance; it was the condition of their hearts.

This prophecy pointed forward to the work of Christ and the indwelling of the Holy Spirit. Salvation is not behavior modification; it's a heart replacement. The stone that could not feel compassion or conviction is exchanged for one that beats with divine rhythm.

If you've ever wondered whether change is possible for you, remember this: God doesn't just cleanse the surface; He rebuilds the core. His Spirit softens what was calloused and ignites what was cold. That's not poetry — that's regeneration.

Reflection

What parts of your heart have gone numb that God is trying to make feel again?

Application

- Ask God to replace indifference with empathy and fear with faith.

- Practice one small act of compassion that stretches your comfort zone.

- When you feel resistant, pray, "Lord, keep my heart soft."

Prayer

Lord, take the stone from my chest and replace it with flesh that feels again. Teach me to love like You — patient, steady, and alive. Amen.

Today's Promise

The heart God gives doesn't just beat differently — it loves differently.

Day 10: A Mind Made New

Scripture

"Do not conform to the pattern of this world but be transformed by the renewing of your mind." — Romans 12:2

Lesson

Paul wrote to the believers in Rome — people surrounded by empire, culture, and comfort that challenged their faith at every turn. His call to "be transformed" came from the Greek word *metamorphoō* — the same root for "metamorphosis."

It described an inward change that produces outward evidence.

The battlefield of transformation is the mind. God doesn't demand blind faith; He invites renewed thinking — thought patterns reshaped by truth. When your mind is aligned with God's Word, your life begins to express His will naturally, not mechanically.

Renewal is not instant, but it's constant. Every day the Spirit rewrites the narratives the world taught you, replacing lies with life.

Reflection

What old thought pattern still speaks louder than God's truth in your mind?

Application

- Replace one recurring negative thought with a verse of Scripture.

- Begin each morning with a gratitude statement instead of a worry.

- Journal how truth changes your outlook by day's end.

Prayer

Lord, reshape my thinking until it reflects Your peace. Renew my mind so I can recognize what is good, pleasing, and perfect in Your will. Amen.

Today's Promise

A renewed mind doesn't escape the world — it transforms it.

Day 11: From Shame to Grace

Scripture

"Those who look to Him are radiant; their faces are never covered with shame." — Psalm 34:5

Lesson

David wrote Psalm 34 after escaping King Achish, pretending to be mad in order to save his life (1 Samuel 21). It was a moment of humiliation and desperation, yet David turned that failure into praise. He discovered that looking to God —

not to pride or performance — brings radiance that no shame can shadow.

Shame tells us to hide; grace tells us to lift our heads. God's love doesn't just erase guilt — it restores worth. The same eyes that once turned away in fear now meet His gaze without flinching. That's the miracle of grace: it doesn't deny what happened; it declares that mercy is stronger.

Reflection

What memory or mistake still tries to define you — even though God has already redeemed it?

Application

- Stand in sunlight today and imagine God's grace shining over your past.
- Say aloud, "I am not my shame; I am God's beloved."
- Extend grace to someone else who carries visible regret.

Prayer

God of grace, lift my face to meet Your eyes. Let Your mercy replace my shame and teach me to shine again. Amen.

Today's Promise

Grace doesn't ignore your story — it rewrites the ending.

Day 12: The Spirit's Seal

Scripture

"When you believed, you were marked in Him with a seal, the promised Holy Spirit." — Ephesians 1:13

Lesson

In the ancient world, a seal was a mark of ownership, authenticity, and protection. Paul used that image to remind believers in Ephesus that faith is not fragile — it's secured by the Spirit Himself. The seal isn't a symbol; it's a Person.

When you said yes to Jesus, heaven stamped you with eternal identity. The Spirit is both the guarantee and the guide — proof that you belong and the power to live like it. You are not forgotten, misplaced, or unsecured. The same Spirit who hovered over creation now dwells in you, completing the good work God began.

Reflection

How would you live differently today if you fully believed you are sealed, protected, and marked as God's own?

Application

- Begin your day declaring, "I am sealed by the Spirit of God."
- When fear whispers, you're alone, remember you carry His presence.
- Let assurance replace anxiety in one area of uncertainty.

Prayer

Holy Spirit, thank You for marking me as Yours. Remind me I'm never unclaimed, never unseen, never unloved. Amen.

Today's Promise

What God seals, no one can steal.

Sunday Reflection: Resting in Renewal

Scripture

"They who wait for the Lord shall renew their strength; they shall mount up with wings like eagles." — Isaiah 40:31

Reflection

Isaiah wrote to people weary from waiting — exiles who feared God had forgotten them. Yet he spoke of a God who does not faint or grow tired, and whose strength is shared with those who trust Him.

Waiting isn't wasted when it's worship. In stillness, strength is restored.

As you sit beside the lake, watching light unfold across the water, remember renewal happens not in motion, but in surrender. God does His best work in the pauses between your strivings.

Joy in the Morning
WEEK 3

Devotionals for the week

Day	Title	Scripture	Theme
13	Joy Comes in the Morning	Psalm 30:5	Hope through hardship
14	Strength in Singing	Nehemiah 8:10	Joy as strength
15	Delight Over Despair	Psalm 37:4	Rejoicing in God's will
16	Joy in Trials	James 1:2	Growth through endurance
17	Fullness of Joy	Psalm 16:11	Presence and peace
18	The Oil of Gladness	Psalm 45:7	Anointed joy
(Sunday)	Resting in Joy	Psalm 16:11	Worshipful stillness

Week 3 Devotionals

Reflect on Joy with this week's special song to accompany the scriptures.

QR Code for Music to Accompany Week 3 Devotionals

Joy in the Morning

Day 13: Joy Comes in the Morning

Scripture

"Weeping may stay for the night, but rejoicing comes in the morning." — Psalm 30:5

Lesson

David wrote this psalm after being delivered from near death — a song of thanksgiving that turns from lament to praise. His life had been a cycle of victory and failure, yet every dark valley ended the same way: with the dawn of mercy.

In Hebrew, the phrase "may stay for the night" implies a temporary guest — grief that visits but does not remain. Joy, however, is the sunrise tenant that moves in permanently. This joy is not naïve optimism; it's resurrection hope. The same God who raised David from despair raises us from the tombs of our own making.

Morning doesn't erase the night — it redeems it. God doesn't promise a life without sorrow, but He does promise that sorrow will never have the final word.

Reflection

Where have you mistaken the silence of night for the absence of God's promise?

Application

- Begin your day by thanking God for one joy that rose after a season of loss.

- Encourage someone still waiting for their dawn.

- When the night feels long, speak Psalm 30:5 aloud until your heart believes it.

Prayer

Lord, thank You that joy is not a feeling that fades with daylight, but a promise that rises with every sunrise. Amen.

Today's Promise

The night may visit, but morning always has the keys.

Day 14: Strength in Singing

Scripture

"Do not grieve, for the joy of the Lord is your strength." — Nehemiah 8:10

Lesson

These words were spoken in Jerusalem as Ezra read the rediscovered Law of God to the people. Hearing it, they began to weep — convicted, overwhelmed, aware of how far they'd drifted. But Nehemiah, their leader, told them not to mourn. This was not a day for regret, but for rejoicing.

Their tears had revealed a tender heart — a sign that God was still at work within them. The joy Nehemiah spoke of wasn't a denial of their brokenness; it was the power to rise beyond it. God's joy doesn't ignore your history — it redeems your heart.

This is the mystery of grace: repentance and joy are not opposites. They are dance partners. The one who grieves sin sincerely finds the deepest reason to rejoice.

Reflection

Do you still see joy as reward, or as strength in the middle of rebuilding?

Application

- When you feel weary, pause and praise before you continue.
- Remember that joy is a weapon — not a luxury.
- Let gratitude be the sound of your resilience.

Prayer

Lord, turn my mourning into melody. Let Your joy strengthen the places in me that have grown tired of starting over. Amen.

Today's Promise

Joy isn't the end of your strength — it's the source of it.

Day 15: Delight Over Despair

Scripture

"Take delight in the Lord, and He will give you the desires of your heart." — Psalm 37:4

Lesson

Psalm 37 was written by David in his later years — a man seasoned by waiting, learning that delight in God was not distraction but direction. When he says, "He will give you the desires of your heart," the Hebrew sense implies transformation: God reshapes your desires until they mirror His.

The delight David describes is not rooted in what God gives, but in who He is. The more you delight in His presence, the more your heart begins to crave holiness over happiness, purpose over possessions.

When life feels unfair, remember that delight does not escape — it's trust in disguise. Joy comes not from getting what we want, but from discovering that in Him, we already have what we need.

Reflection

What are you desiring today that might need God's refining touch?

Application

- Spend five minutes in silent adoration — not asking, just enjoying God's presence.

- Replace frustration with gratitude in one area of waiting.

- Write down how your desires have changed since walking with Him.

Prayer

Father, shape my heart to want what You want. Let delight be my compass and joy my reward. Amen.

Today's Promise

When God becomes your delight, your heart will never lack direction.

Day 16: Joy in Trials

Scripture

"Consider it pure joy, my brothers and sisters, whenever you face trials of many kinds." — James 1:2

Lesson

James, the half-brother of Jesus, wrote to early believers scattered by persecution. They had lost homes, security, and community. Yet he told them to "consider it joy" — not because suffering feels good, but because it forms something good: endurance.

The Greek word for "consider" means to lead your thoughts — to direct your mind toward truth rather than default to despair. Trials do not define your faith; they refine it. The heat that burns away comfort also forges strength.

Joy in trials is not denial — it's defiance. It looks suffering in the eye and says, "You will not have the final say."

Reflection

What challenge are you facing that God might be using to produce something eternal?

Application

- When hardship comes, ask, "What are You forming in me through this?"
- Choose gratitude in one difficulty this week.
- Encourage someone walking through a valley — be their reminder that endurance has purpose.

Prayer

Lord, teach me to find joy not after the trial, but within it. Turn my pain into perseverance and my fear into faith. Amen.

Today's Promise

Joy isn't found after the trial — it's forged inside it.

Day 17: Fullness of Joy

Scripture

"In Your presence there is fullness of joy; at Your right hand are pleasures forevermore." — Psalm 16:11

Lesson

Psalm 16 is a declaration of trust written by David during uncertainty and danger. He rejoices not in his circumstances but in his proximity to God. The phrase "fullness of joy" points to completion — a joy that lacks nothing because it springs from being with the One who lacks nothing.

This psalm is also prophetic: Peter later quotes it in Acts 2, applying it to Jesus' resurrection. True joy finds its source not in temporary relief but in eternal victory. To dwell in God's presence is to step into a space where fear loses its vocabulary and hope becomes native language.

The world offers happiness in pieces; God offers joy in wholeness.

Reflection

Where do you go seeking joy that can only be found in His presence?

Application

- Begin your prayer time today with worship rather than requests.

- Pause to notice one sign of God's nearness — nature, music, kindness.

- Ask Him to fill the empty spaces joy alone can occupy.

Prayer

God of joy, let Your presence fill every shadow in me. May my heart echo eternity even in ordinary moments. Amen.

Today's Promise

The presence of God doesn't add joy to your life — it becomes your life's joy.

Day 18: The Oil of Gladness

Scripture

"You love righteousness and hate wickedness; therefore God, your God, has anointed you with the oil of gladness beyond your companions." — Psalm 45:7

Lesson

Psalm 45 was a royal wedding song that the writer of Hebrews later applied to Jesus (Hebrews 1:9). The "oil of gladness" symbolizes anointing — divine favor, empowerment, and joy that comes from God's approval. Christ was anointed above all others because His obedience was perfect and His love unblemished.

When you walk in alignment with God's will, that same anointing of gladness flows through you. Joy becomes more than emotion; it becomes evidence of intimacy with the King.

Gladness is not naïveté; it's the fragrance of righteousness. The closer you stay to His heart, the more your countenance carries the scent of heaven.

Reflection

What would change if you saw joy not as optional, but as part of your anointing?

Application

- Ask God to restore the joy that obedience brings.
- Smile intentionally at someone today — let gladness become ministry.
- Thank Him for the quiet confidence that comes from walking rightly.

Prayer

Lord, anoint me with Your gladness. Let joy mark my life as proof of Your Spirit's presence. Amen.

Today's Promise

Joy is not decoration — it's evidence of divine anointing.

Sunday Reflection: Resting in Joy

Scripture

"In Your presence there is fullness of joy." — Psalm 16:11

Reflection

Sabbath joy is not noise or celebration — it's contentment.

Joy rests as easily as it rises. As you sit beside still water or watch the shimmer of light across the lake, remember: the same God who fills you with strength also fills you with serenity.

The week's labors and songs have poured out — now, breathe in grace.

Rest is not the absence of worship; it is worship in stillness.

Smile, exhale, and remember: joy continues long after the song is over.

Hope and Light for a New Day

WEEK 4

Devotionals for the week

Day	Title	Scripture	Theme
19	Hope That Anchors	Hebrews 6:19	Stability and faith
20	Light in Darkness	John 1:5	Christ's overcoming light
21	The Morning Star	Revelation 22:16	Promise of His return
22	Future Glory	Romans 8:18	Perspective in suffering
23	Mercy and Compassion	Psalm 145:9	God's goodness for all
24	Radiant with Hope	Psalm 34:5	Hope reflected outward
(Sunday)	Resting in Hope	Matthew 11:28	Surrender and peace

Week 4 Devotionals

Scan here to listen to a song chosen for this week's devotionals.

QR Code for Music to Accompany Week 4 Devotionals

Sunrise over the lake

Day 19: Hope That Anchors

Scripture

"We have this hope as an anchor for the soul, firm and secure." — Hebrews 6:19

Lesson

The writer of Hebrews was encouraging believers who were tempted to drift back toward old ways and tired, persecuted, and uncertain about the unseen future.

He reminded them that God's promises to Abraham were not conditional; they were sealed with an oath God swore by His own name. That promise became their anchor — not in calm waters, but amid storms.

Hope in Scripture is not wishful thinking. It is confident expectation built on God's unchanging character. An anchor doesn't stop the waves; it keeps the vessel steady when the waves rise. Faith may strain, but hope holds.

In your own seasons of turbulence, remember: the same God who anchored Abraham's descendants in covenant keeps you secure in Christ. When the world shifts, His word does not.

Reflection

What storms in your life tempt you to lift your anchor and drift?

Application

- Write down one promise from Scripture that has kept you steady.

- When worry rises, declare aloud, "My hope is anchored in Christ."

- Encourage someone else who feels adrift by sharing a promise that steadies you.

Prayer

Lord, in the rise and fall of life's tides, hold me fast to Your promise. Let hope be my anchor, firm and secure in You. Amen.

Today's Promise

Hope doesn't calm the sea — it keeps you steady in the storm.

Day 20: Light in Darkness

Scripture

"The light shines in the darkness, and the darkness has not overcome it." — John 1:5

Lesson

John's gospel opens not with Bethlehem but with eternity. Before creation began, the Word — Christ — already was. His light pierced a formless world then, and it pierces our darkness now. John's readers faced persecution and doubt;

he reminded them that darkness can resist light, but it can never defeat it.

Light in Scripture represents revelation — truth that exposes lies and leads the lost home. Christ's light doesn't merely reveal; it renews. The night has no choice but to yield when He enters the room.

Even in your dimmest seasons, remember darkness is not the absence of God's work — it's the canvas upon which His glory shines brightest.

Reflection

Where has God's light recently broken through in your life, even if only as a faint glimmer?

Application

- Start your morning by turning on a light and whispering John 1:5 aloud.

- Replace one fear-based thought with gratitude for what God has revealed.

- Be a light-bearer: speak encouragement where others see only gloom.

Prayer

Light of the world, illuminate my doubts, dispel my fears, and let Your truth shine through me today. Amen.

Today's Promise

The smallest light still defeats the deepest dark.

Day 21: The Morning Star

Scripture

"I am the Root and the Offspring of David, the bright Morning Star." — Revelation 22:16

Lesson

John received this revelation on the island of Patmos — exiled, isolated, and yet given a glimpse of eternity. In the final chapter of Scripture, Jesus identifies Himself as the "Morning Star" — the light that signals the end of night and the promise of a new dawn.

In ancient times, the morning star appeared just before sunrise, heralding the coming of light. Christ's return will do the same on a cosmic scale. But even now, His presence in you is that same morning star — hope glowing against the horizon of a weary world.

When you see the faint light of dawn, remember: Jesus is already shining in the distance. Night can only last until He rises.

Reflection

How does knowing that Christ is the Morning Star change the way you face long nights?

Application

- Watch one sunrise this week and thank God for this promise fulfilled daily.
- Pray for those still living in spiritual night to see His light breaking through.
- Let anticipation, not anxiety, define your waiting.

Prayer

Bright Morning Star, shine through the darkness of our time and through the shadows of my heart. Your coming light is my living hope. Amen.

Today's Promise

Every sunrise is a whisper that the Morning Star still shines.

Day 22: Future Glory

Scripture

"I consider that our present sufferings are not worth comparing with the glory that will be revealed in us." — Romans 8:18

Lesson

Paul wrote this to believers in Rome who faced daily persecution. His message was not a denial of pain but a redirection of perspective. Suffering, he explained, is not meaningless —

it's preparation. The glory to come doesn't erase the wounds; it redeems them.

The Greek word *doxa* for "glory" conveys radiance — light revealed. Paul believed that the light within us, though veiled by pain now, would one day break forth with brilliance. What feels like pressure today is the hand of the Potter shaping eternal beauty.

Your present story may ache, but its ending is radiant. Earth's shadows will fade; heaven's dawn will rise — and in that light, you will understand why every dark valley was worth crossing.

Reflection

What current hardship might be preparing you for something more beautiful than you can yet imagine?

Application

- Journal how a past trial has produced present strength or empathy.

- When pain feels pointless, pray, "Show me the glory You're forming through this."

- Encourage a friend by reminding them their suffering is not the story's end.

Prayer

God of future glory, help me see today through the lens of eternity. May every tear become a reflection of Your coming joy. Amen.

Today's Promise

Present pain is the shadow; glory is the sunrise behind it.

Day 23: Mercy and Compassion

Scripture

"The Lord is good to all; He has compassion on all He has made." — Psalm 145:9

Lesson

Psalm 145 is David's final psalm — a sweeping declaration of God's goodness to all creation. Written by a man who had tasted triumph and tragedy alike, it testifies that mercy is not seasonal; it's structural to God's character. His compassion isn't reserved for the deserving — it flows to the entire world He formed.

David's closing song is not naïve; it's the voice of experience. He had sinned grievously, been restored mercifully, and learned that God's compassion is stronger than human frailty. The same mercy that met David still meets you — not once, but daily.

Reflection

Who around you most need to see God's compassion reflected through you?

Application

- Extend kindness today to someone outside your comfort zone.
- When tempted to judge, remember how freely God has shown you mercy.
- End your day by thanking Him for one act of compassion you witnessed.

Prayer

Merciful Father, let my heart mirror Yours. Teach me to show compassion as freely as I've received it. Amen.

Today's Promise

God's mercy is not limited — it's limitless.

Day 24: Radiant with Hope

Scripture

"Those who look to Him are radiant; their faces are never covered with shame." — Psalm 34:5

Lesson

David sang these words after escaping danger, praising the God who had turned fear into radiance. To "look to Him" meant to fix the gaze of trust, not just a passing glance. When eyes turn upward, countenance changes. Shame melts where hope begins.

The radiance David describes is not physical — it's the inner glow of those who know they are seen and loved by God. In a world dimmed by despair, the light of hope is the most striking testimony you can carry.

Let your life reflect what your heart believes: that the God who saves also shines through those He's redeemed.

Reflection

What part of your story could shine brighter if you stopped hiding it in shame?

Application

- Smile intentionally today — not as performance, but as reflection.

- Share one testimony of God's faithfulness with someone who needs hope.

- When fear darkens your thoughts, lift your face toward His light.

Prayer

Lord, make me radiant with Your hope. Let others see Your reflection when they look my way. Amen.

Today's Promise

Hope on the inside always shows on the outside.

Sunday Reflection: Resting in Hope

Scripture

"Come to Me, all you who are weary and burdened, and I will give you rest." — Matthew 11:28

Reflection

Hope is not a restless reach; it's a restful trust. The same God who calls you to act in faith also calls you to sit in assurance. When you come to Him weary, He doesn't demand effort — He offers ease.

At Amané, the morning light on the lake is not hurried. It arrives softly, steadily, faithfully. That's how hope comes too — not always in flashes, but in quiet certainty. Let this day be your exhale. You are held. You are heard. You are home in His hope.

Living the Promise
WEEK 5

Devotionals for the week

Day	Title	Scripture	Theme
25	Walking in the Light	1 John 1:7	Living truthfully
26	Faith in Action	James 2:17	Active belief
27	The Peaceful Path	Philippians 4:9	Practicing peace
28	Bearing Fruit That Lasts	John 15:16	Lasting impact
29	The Strength of Service	Galatians 6:9	Persevering love
30	Abiding in Love	John 15:9–10	Ongoing communion
(Sunday)	Resting in Promise	Hebrews 4:9–10	Renewal through rest
31	The Promise Continues	Psalm 23:6	Renewal without end

Week 5 Devotionals

Scan to listen to a song that inspires us to walk daily in God's promise.

QR Code for Music to accompany Week 5 Devotionals

Hope and Light for a New Day

Day 25: Walking in the Light

Scripture

"If we walk in the light, as He is in the light, we have fellowship with one another, and the blood of Jesus, His Son, purifies us from all sin." — 1 John 1:7

Lesson

John wrote to a church struggling with division and false teaching — a people tempted to separate belief from behavior. His reminder was clear: to walk in the light means not just to believe in Christ, but to live in His truth.

In the Greek, "walk" implies continuous motion — a daily rhythm of transparency and obedience. The light of Christ doesn't just expose sin; it invites community and cleansing. To walk in the light is to live without pretense, letting grace do its daily work.

At Amané, dawn never rushes. It moves steadily across the water, lighting every hidden place. That's how God's light works in us — slow enough to heal, bright enough to change.

Reflection

What would your next step look like if you walked completely in the light today?

Application

- Confess, don't conceal — bring one hidden burden into prayer or accountability.

- Let honesty become a form of worship.

- Thank God for the fellowship that grows in the light of grace.

Prayer

Lord, guide my steps in Your light. Keep me transparent, teachable, and true. Let my life reflect Your brightness in every shadowed place. Amen.

Today's Promise

The light that cleanses also connects.

Day 26: Faith in Action

Scripture

"Faith by itself, if it is not accompanied by action, is dead." — James 2:17

Lesson

James wrote to believers who had grown comfortable in confession but complacent in compassion. His letter isn't a contradiction to grace; it's a confirmation of it. True faith inevitably produces visible fruit — not to earn God's love, but to express it.

The Greek word for "dead" (*nekros*) means lifeless, without motion. Faith without action is like a sunrise you never open the blinds to see. Belief alone can acknowledge God; obedience reveals Him.

Action doesn't make faith real — it makes faith *seen*. Every time you serve, forgive, or give, the unseen becomes visible.

Reflection

Where might God be calling you to turn belief into movement this week?

Application

- Meet a need quietly and practically — no spotlight, just service.

- Write a note of encouragement or reconciliation.

- Let compassion interrupt your schedule.

Prayer

Lord, awaken my faith into action. Let my hands speak what my heart believes. Make love my language and service my song. Amen.

Today's Promise

Living faith doesn't wait to feel ready — it moves in trust.

Day 27: The Peaceful Path

Scripture

"Whatever you have learned or received or heard from me—or seen in me—put it into practice. And the God of peace will be with you." — Philippians 4:9

Lesson

Paul wrote from prison, yet his words overflow with peace. To the Philippians, he gave a formula not for escape, but for embodiment: practice what you know to be true, and peace will follow.

Peace in Scripture isn't merely the absence of conflict; it's *shalom* — wholeness, harmony, alignment with God's will. The secret is obedience: peace isn't found, it's practiced.

At Amané, the lake's stillness reflects the sky only when undisturbed. Likewise, the soul reflects God's peace when trust stills the waters of worry.

Reflection

What would practicing peace look like in the middle of your current stress?

Application

- Choose one response today that trades control for calm.

- Turn complaint into gratitude; replace reaction with prayer.

- Pursue reconciliation where tension remains.

Prayer

God of peace, teach me the rhythm of stillness in motion.

Let calmness become my courage and kindness my defense.

Amen.

Today's Promise

Peace doesn't arrive …

it abides with those who practice it.

Day 28: Bearing Fruit That Lasts

Scripture

"I chose you and appointed you so that you might go and bear fruit—fruit that will last." — John 15:16

Lesson

On the night before His crucifixion, Jesus spoke these words to His disciples. He was preparing them not for ease, but endurance. The fruit He described wasn't momentary success — it was eternal impact born from abiding relationship.

"Fruit that lasts" comes from remaining connected to the Vine. It doesn't rot because it's rooted in His Spirit, not our strength. This kind of fruit looks like love that forgives quickly, joy that outlasts grief, and faith that keeps sowing even when the harvest is unseen.

The proof of discipleship isn't performance; it's perseverance.

Reflection

What kind of fruit is your life producing right now — temporary or lasting?

Application

- Invest in one act of love that may not return immediate results.
- Prioritize abiding overachieving in your prayer life today.
- Thank God for every unseen seed that is quietly growing.

Prayer

Lord, prune what hinders my fruitfulness. Let every branch of my life glorify You through enduring love.

Amen.

Today's Promise

Fruit that lasts grows from roots that rest.

Day 29: The Strength of Service

Scripture

"Let us not become weary in doing good, for at the proper time we will reap a harvest if we do not give up." — Galatians 6:9

Lesson

Paul's letter to the Galatians came near the end of a long ministry marked by hardship. He knew that even good work can grow heavy. The call to perseverance was not about productivity but partnership — sharing in Christ's endurance for the sake of others.

Service, in God's kingdom, is not measured by outcome but by faithfulness. Every unseen act of kindness builds an invisible harvest.

The timing belongs to God, but the calling belongs to you.

When fatigue whispers "stop," listen for the quieter voice that says "steady." Even when you can't see results, heaven keeps count.

Reflection

Where are you tempted to give up on something God never asked you to finish alone?

Application

- Revisit a task or relationship you've abandoned in exhaustion — pray before deciding it's over.
- Offer gratitude to someone who serves quietly and consistently.
- Choose rest, not resignation.

Prayer

Lord, strengthen my hands for service and my heart for endurance. Let me sow faithfully, trusting You with the harvest.

Amen.

Today's Promise

Heaven never overlooks faithful hands.

Day 30: Abiding in Love

Scripture

"As the Father has loved Me, so have I loved you. Now remain in My love." — John 15:9

Lesson

Jesus spoke these words just before His arrest — an intimate invitation to dwell, not just believe. The command to "remain" means to make a home in His love — to let it become the atmosphere of your existence.

Love is the soil where every other virtue grows. Without it, even the best intentions wither. Abiding love is not mere sentiment; it's steady surrender — a daily returning to the Source.

The Father's love for Jesus was perfect, unbroken, and eternal — and that is the same love extended to you. The command to remain is not a restriction; it's a refuge.

Reflection

Are you resting in God's love, or striving to earn what's already yours?

Application

- Begin the day with quiet acknowledgment: *"I am loved by God, and that is enough."*

- Let your next conversation, decision, or response flow from that love.

- End your day by reflecting on how His love held you steady.

Prayer

Jesus, teach me to remain.

Let Your love be my dwelling place, my rest, and my rhythm.

Amen.

Today's Promise

The one who abides in love never runs out of light.

Sunday Reflection: Resting in Promise

Scripture

"There remains, then, a Sabbath rest for the people of God." — Hebrews 4:9

Reflection

As you close this fifth week, rest is not the end of the journey — it's its fulfillment. Every act of service, every seed of love, every sunrise of hope finds its completion in God's presence. The promise isn't just for tomorrow; it's peace for today.

At Amané, when the lake is still and the last light glows on the water, you can almost hear creation breathe. Let your soul breathe too.

You've walked with God through mercy, renewal, joy, and hope — now live in His promise, steady and sure.

Day 31: The Promise Continues

Scripture

"Surely goodness and mercy shall follow me all the days of my life, and I will dwell in the house of the Lord forever." — Psalm 23:6

Lesson

The journey doesn't end on the thirtieth sunrise—it begins again. God's promises don't expire when the page turns; they pursue you into tomorrow. Each sunrise is not a repeat but a renewal, a new invitation to walk with Him in trust and peace.

David's words remind us that God's mercy doesn't wait for morning—it *follows* us, relentlessly, even through the valleys and shadows. The same grace that carried you through these thirty days will carry you through the rest of your life.

When the devotional ends, the dialogue continues. God still speaks, still restores, still renews. The sun that rose today will rise again tomorrow—not because the world demands it, but because God delights in bringing light.

Reflection

You've spent thirty days learning to meet God at dawn, to see His hand in your mornings, and to trust His faithfulness through each season. Now, you walk forward not as a reader, but as a *witness*—someone who knows that the promise of renewal is not bound by a book, but by the heart of God.

Application

- Begin tomorrow as you did on Day 1: expectant, thankful, awake to grace.
- Share one truth or verse from this devotional with someone who needs it.
- Ask God what "new promise" He wants to show you next.

Prayer

Father, thank You that Your goodness and mercy don't end with the last page. They follow me into every new morning.

Help me keep meeting You there— in stillness, in Scripture, in the rhythm of daily trust. Let my life be a living continuation of Your promise. In Jesus' name, Amen.

Tomorrow's Promise

The story of grace doesn't end—it rises again every morning.

Scan here to learn more about the Amané House:

Learn more about the Amané House

ABOUT THE AUTHOR

Ever since I accepted Jesus Christ at a church camp when I was 16, I've known deep in my heart that God is real. But for much of my life, I treated Him like a silent partner in the shadows—someone I would thank when things went well in business or life, and someone I would reason with when I made compromises, hoping that being a "mostly good person" was good enough.

But that's not how it works.

You don't get a pass for walking with God some of the time. A true relationship with Him is not a part-time belief—it's a full-time surrender. Through the grace of God, He never stopped reaching for me. He placed people in my life—especially a couple of pastors—who challenged me to mature in my faith and helped me better understand what it means to walk daily with Christ.

And perhaps more quietly, but just as powerfully, my wife Alma has been instrumental in that growth. Her strength, perspective, and unwavering faith have made me more introspective about my actions and my relationship with God. Her example of quiet trust and spiritual clarity has helped me grow in ways I never expected—and always needed.

I've always loved sunrises. They've symbolized new beginnings for me—fresh hope, fresh light, and a fresh promise. With the encouragement of the people God placed in my path, and with the tools of today—research, technology, and even AI—I set out to explore how the sunrise could reflect something far deeper: God's continual invitation to renewal.

That's why I wrote this book. I pray it shows others what I've come to understand: that every single morning, God offers not just another day, but another chance. He invites us into relationship, trust, hope—and transformation. Not part-time. Not performative. But real, eternal, and full.

— Kevin Brady

www.ingramcontent.com/pod-product-compliance
Lightning Source LLC
LaVergne TN
LVHW050625090426
835512LV00007B/663